FIRST LADIES OF
USA

FIRST LADIES OF
USA

Part 1

Marshella Marshall

FIRST LADIES OF USA
PART 1

iUniverse books may be ordered through booksellers or by contacting:

iUniverse
1663 Liberty Drive
Bloomington, IN 47403
www.iuniverse.com
844-349-9409

ISBN: 978-1-5320-7623-7 (sc)
ISBN: 978-1-5320-7624-4 (e)

Library of Congress Control Number: 2019906700

Print information available on the last page.

iUniverse rev. date: 03/09/2021

1ˢᵗ President Wife

Martha Dandbridge Curtis Washington
Born: June 2, 1731 Chestnut Grove New Kent County, Virginia
Mother: France Jones Dandbridge
Father: John Dandbridge
Marriage: 1759 Colonel George Washington (1732-99)
Children: Daniel Custis (1751-56), Frances Custis (1753-57),
John 'Jacky' Custis (1755-81) and Martha 'Patsy' Custis (1757-73)

Martha washington

June 13, 1731 – May 22, 1802

2ⁿᵈ **President Wife**

Abigail Quincy Smith Adams
Born: November 11, 1744 Weymouth, Massachusetts
Died: October 28, 1818, Quincy Massachusetts
Mother: Elizabeth Quincy Smith
Father: Reverend William Smith
First Marriage: 1764 to John Adams
Children: Abigail 'Nabby" Amelia (1765-1813), John Quincy (1767-1848, Susana (1768-70), Charles (1770-1800), and Thomas Boylston (1772-1732)

Abigail Adams
November 22, 1744 – October 28, 1818

3rd President Wife

Martha Wayless Skelton Jefferson
Born: October 1748 Charles City County, Virginia
Died: September 6, 1782 Monticello, Virginia
Mother: Martha Eppess Wayless
Father: John Wayless
First Marriage: 1766 to Barthurst Skelton, 1768(d)
Remarried: Thomas Jefferson 1772-1826
Children: Martha 'Patsy' Jane Randolph, unnamed son, Maria 'Polly', and Elizabeth

4th President Wife

Dolley Payne Todd Madison
Born: May 20, 1768 New Garden, Quaker Settlement, North Carolina
Died: July 12, 1849 Washington DC
Mother: Mary Coles Payne
Father: John Payne
Children: John Payne Todd (1792-1852), William Temple Todd (1793-93)

Dolley Madison
May 20, 1768 – July 12, 1849

5th President Wife

Elizabeth Kortright Monroe
Born: June 30, 1768 New York, New York
Died: September 23, 1830, Loundon County, Virginia
Mother: Hannah Aspenwall Kortright
Father: Captain Lawrence Kortright
First marriage: February 16, 1786 to James Monroe
Children: Eliza (1786-1840) James Spence (1799-1801) Maria
Hester (1803-50)

6th President Wife

Louisa Catherine Johnson Adams

Born: February 12, 1775, London England

Died: May 15, 1852, Washington DC

Mother: Catherine Nuth Johnson

Father: Joshua Johnson

First Marriage: July 26, 1997 to John Quincy Adams (1769-1848)

Children: George Washington (1801-29) John II (1803-34) Charles Francis (1807-86) Louisa Catherine (1811-12?)

Louisa Adams

February 12, 1775 – May 15, 1852

7th President Wife

Rachel Donelson Robards Jackson
Born: June 15, 1767, Halifax County, Virginia
Died: December 22, 1828, Nashville, Tennessee
Mother: Rachel Stockeley Donelson
Father: Colonel John Donelson
First Marriage: 1785, Lewis Robards
Remarried: 1791, Andrew Jackson (1767-1845)
Children: Andrew Jackson Donelson, The adopted son. 1809-
Lyncoya, Creek Indian Boy and raised nieces and nephews

Emily Donelson
June 1, 1807 – December 19, 1836

8th President Wife

Hannah Van Buren
Born: March 8 1783, Kinderhook, New York
Died: February 5, 1819, Albany, New York
Mother: Maria Quachenboss Hoes
Father: John Dirchsen Hoes
First Marriage: Martin Van Buren, February 21, 1807-1862
Children: Abraham (1807-73) John (1801-66) Martin (1812-55) Winfield Scott (1814) Smith Thompson (1817-76)

ngelica Singleton Van Bure
February 13, 1818 – December 29, 1877

9th President Wife

Anna Tuthill Symmes Harrison
Born: July 26, 1775
Died: February 25, 1864, North Bend, Ohio
Mother: Anna Tuthill Symmes
Father: Judge John Cleves
First Marriage: November 25, 1795
Remarried: William Henry Harrison (1773-1841)
Children: Elizabeth Bassett (1796-1846) John Cleves Symmes (1798-1830) Lucy Singleton (1800-26) William Henryll (1802-38) John Scott (1804-78) Benjamin (1806-40) Mary Symmes (1809-42) Carter Basset (1813-45) Anna Tuthill (1813-45) James Findlay (18-14-17)

Anna Harrison
July 25, 1775 – February 25, 1864

10th President Wife

Letitia Christian Tyler
Born: November 12, 1790, Cedar Grove Plantation near Richmond, Virginia
Died: September 10, 1842, Washington DC
Mother: Mary Browne Christian
Father: Robert Christian
First marriage: March 29, 1813, John Tyler (1790-1862)
Children: Mary (1815-48) Robert (1816-77) John Jr. (1819-96) Letitia (1821-1907) Elizabeth (1823-50)
Anne Contesse (1825) Alice (1827-54) Tazewell (1830-74)

Pricilla Cooper Tyler
June 14, 1816 – December 29, 1889

11th President Wife

Sarah Childless Polk
Born: September 4, 1803, Murfreesboro, Tennessee
Died: August 4, 1891, Nashville, Tennessee
Mother: Elizabeth Whitsett Childless
Father: Joel Childless
First Marriage: January 1, 1824 to James K. Polk (1795-1849)
Children: none

Sarah Childress Polk
September 4, 1803 – August 14, 1891

12th President Wife

Margaret Mackall Smith Taylor
Born: September 21, 1788 Calvert County, Maryland
Died: August 14, 1852, East Pascagoula, Mississippi
Mother: Ann Mackall Smith
Father: Walter Smith
First Marriage: June 21, 1810 to Zachary Taylor (1784-1850)
Children: Ann Margaret Mackall (1811-75) Sarah Knox (1814-35) Octavia Pannel (1816-20) Margaret Smith (1819-20) Mary Elizabeth 'Betty' (1824-1909), Richard (1826-79)

Margaret Mackall Smith
September 21, 1788 – August 14, 1852

13th President Wife

Abigail Powers Filmore
Born: March 13, 1798, Saragota County, New York
Died: March 30, 1853, Washinton DC
Mother: Abigail Newland Powers
Father: Reverend Lemeul Powers
First Marriage: February 5, 1826 Millard Filmore (1800-74)
Children: Millard Powers (1828-89) Mary Abigail (1832-54)

14th President Wife

Jane Means Appleton Pierce
Born: March 12, 1806 Hampton, New Hamspire
Died: December 2, 1863 Andover, Massachusetts
Mother: Elizabeth Means Appleton
Father: Reverend Jesse Appleton
First Marriage: November 19, 1834 to Franklin Pierce (1804-69)
Children: Franklin Jr. (1836) Fran Robert (1839-43) Benjamin (1841-53)

Jane Pierce
March 12, 1806 – December 2, 1863

15th President Wife

Harriet Rebecca Lane Johnson
Born: May 18, 1830 Mecersburg, Pennsylvania
Died: July 3, 1903 Narragansett, Rhode Island
Mother: Jane Buchanan Lane
Father: Elliot Tole Lane
First Marriage: January 11, 1866 to Henry Elliot Johnson
(1866-1884)
Children: James Buchanan Johnston (1868-81) Henry Elliot
Johnson (1869-82)

Harriet Lane
May 9, 1830 – July 3, 1903

16th President Wife

Mary Ann Todd Lincoln
Born: December 13, 1818, Lexington, Kentucky
Died: July 16, 1882, Springfield, Illinois
Mother: Eliza Ann Parker
Step mom: Elizabeth Humphrey
Father: Robert Smith Todd
First marriage: November 4, 18452 to Abraham Lincoln (1809-65)
Children: Robert Todd (1843-1926) Edward Baker (1846-50) William Wallace (1850-62) Thomas (1853-71)

Mary Todd Lincoln

December 13, 1818 – July 16, 1882

17ᵗʰ President Wife

Eliza McCardle Johnson
Born: October 4, 1810 Leesburg, Tennessee
Died: January 15, 1876 Carter Station, Tennessee
Mother: Sarah Phillips McCardle
Father: John McCardle
First Marriage: May 17, 1827 Andrew Johnson (1808-75)
Childre: Martha (1828-1901) Charles (1830-63) Mary (1832-83) Robert (1834-69) Andrew, Jr, Frank (1852-69)

Eliza Mcardle Johnson
October 4, 1810 – January 15, 1876

18th President Wife

Julia Dent Grant
Born: January 26, 1826 near St. Louis, Missouri
Died: December 14, 1902 Wahsington DC
Mother: Ellen Bray Wrenshall Dent
Father: Frederick Dent
First Marriage: August 22, 1848 to Ulysses S. Grant (1822-85)
Children: Frederick Dent (1850-1912) Ulysses Simpson 'Buck' Jr. (1852-1928) Ellen 'Nellie' Wrenshall (1855-1922) Jesse Root (1858-1934)

Julia Grant
January 26, 1826 – December 14, 1902

19th President Wife

Lucy Ware Webb Hayes

Born: August 28, 1831 Chillicothe, Ohio

Died: June 25, 1889 Fremont, Ohio

Mother: Maria Cook Webb

Father: Dr. James Webb

First Marriage: December 30, 1852 Rutherford Richard Hayes

Children: Birchard Austin (1853-1926) Webb Cook (1858-1927) Joseph Thompson (1861-63) George Crook (1864-66) Fanny (1867-1950) Scott Russell (1871-1923) Manning Force (1873-74)

20th President Wife

Lucretia Rudolph Garfield
Born: April 19, 1832 Garrestsville, Ohio
Died: March 14, 1918 South Pasadena, California
Mother: Arabella Mason Rudolph
Father: Zebulon Rudolph
First Marriage: November 11, 1858 James Abram Garfield
Children: Eliza 'Trot' Arabella (1860-63) Harry Augustus (1865-1950) Mary 'Mollie' (18-67-1947) Irvin McDowell (1870-1951) Abram (1872-1958) Edward 'Neddie' (1874-76)

Lucretia Garfield
April 19, 1832 – March 14, 1918

21st President Wife

Ellen Lewis Herndon Arthur
Born: August 30, 1837, Culpepper County, Virginia
Died: January 12, 1990 New York, New York
Mother: Frances Elizabeth Hansbrough Herndon
Father: Captain William Lewis Herndon
First Marriage: October 25, 1859 Chester Arthur (1829-86)
Children: William Lewis Herndon (1860-63) Chester Allanii
(1864-1937) Ellen Herndon (1871-1915)

Mary Arthur McElroy
July 5, 1841 – January 8, 1917

Printed in the United States
by Baker & Taylor Publisher Services